DESTROYER OF NAIVETÉS

DESTROYER OF NAIVETÉS

Joseph Nechvatal

punctum books (P) brooklyn, ny

DESTROYER OF NAIVETÉS
© Joseph Nechvatal, 2015.

http://creativecommons.org/licenses/by-nc-sa/4.0/

This work carries a Creative Commons BY-NC-SA 4.0 International license, which means that you are free to copy and redistribute the material in any medium or format, and you may also remix, transform and build upon the material, as long as you clearly attribute the work to the authors (in a way that does not suggest the authors or punctum endorse you and your work), you do not use this work for commercial gain in any form whatsoever, and that for any remixing and transformation, you distribute your rebuild under the same license.

First published in 2015 by
punctum books
Brooklyn, New York
http://punctumbooks.com

punctum books is an independent, open-access publisher dedicated to radically creative modes of intellectual inquiry and writing across a whimsical para-humanities assemblage. We solicit and pimp quixotic, sagely mad engagements with textual thought-bodies. We provide shelters for intellectual vagabonds.

Cover Image: Joseph Nechvatal, *penelOpe in agOny* (2014), 44 in. x 66 in. computer-robotic-assisted acrylic on velour canvas. Courtesy of Galerie Richard Paris / New York. Book design by Jake Valente.

ISBN-13: 978-0692573129
ISBN-10: 0692573127

Facing-page illustration by Heather Masciandaro.

Table of Contents

Introduction • i

Destroyer of Naivetés

I • 1
II • 5
III • 17
IV • 27
V • 39
VI • 61
VII • 79
VIII • 87
IX • 91

Acknowledgments • 97

Introduction

DESTROYER OF NAIVETÉS

In a society that believes that the less you conceal, the stranger you become—in a culture where surveillance/intrusion is tied to our drive for self-revealing everything (an antiprivate life culture of curiosity, egotism, solitude, fear, voyeurism, exhibitionism and resentment, where the feeling is that nothing could or should remain unknown to us)—I give you *Destroyer of Naivetés*.

Although I have been sporadically (and mostly secretly) writing poetry for most of my adult life, the poem *Destroyer of Naivetés* really began with my first dabbling in farce literature. This would be my 1995 cyber-sex novella *~~~~~~~~~~~~~~~~~~venus©-~Ñ~vibrator, even*. I wrote *venus* during my artist residency at the Cité des Art International in Paris during 1995, when I was lovesick. I edited it to its final version in New York City in 1999. A portion was presented via audio computer reading as part of my exhibition *vOluptuary : an algorithmic hermaphornology* that was held at Universal Concepts Unlimited Gallery in New York City during the spring of 2003. A very limited-edition audio

CD version of it was produced by Arcane Device (David Lee Myers) featuring Myers's music.

Paris is deeply implicated here. In 1995 I came to Paris from New York to live for the first time, up in Montmartre. There I felt it my duty to read all of Henry Miller's books that dealt with sex. That led me inevitably to Anaïs Nin's book on sex, *Delta of Venus*. I had already read all of Jean Genet's work and his style marked me deeply. In New York I had become something of an aficionado of Marcel Duchamp's *The Bride Stripped Bare by Her Bachelors, Even* (*La mariée mise à nu par ses célibataires, même*), the drawings of Hans Bellmer, films and performances of my comrade Bradley Eros, and the erotic scribblings of Giacomo Casanova, Georges Bataille, Petronius, Erica Jong, Vladimir Nabokov, Marquis de Sade, Yukio Mishima, Ovid, Leopold von Sacher-Masoch, and Kathy Acker. Indeed, Acker's wild snatch style urged me on to try my own hand at sex farce.

But my grubby theme of male sexual memory and fantasy fully blossomed for me as pitiable poetry after exchanging poetic fragments with Robert C. Morgan in 2009 (I love his hysterical poems). All of this was finally coupled with my joyful reading of *I Am a Beautiful Monster* by Francis Picabia (translated by Marc Lowenthal). Picabia really got his nails into me, and I took his hint. Thus I began *Destroyer of Naivetés* by first scavenging some particularly satisfactory phrases from ~~~~~~~~~~~~~~~~~~*venus©-~Ñ~vibrator, even*. That is what got me going on this epic poem. One I was determined to finish by May 22, 2013 as a gift to my wife Marie-Claude. And so it was.

Paris, France
2015

I

Of Please Keep Your Eyes On

eyes elaborately punctuated with placid lakes
eyes strewn with a profusion of gay flowers
eyes strange with a tinge of soft radiance

eyes
flared phallic-like
pompadour eye

in fifth terrace semi-circular configuration
eyes dance strewn with irises, roses, daffodils
with miniature grotesquely attenuated satyrs

eyes festooned
genitals in hand with dainty petticoats

lust dripping white wax
blue and white veined marble eyes
extravagant fruits and flowers

hung about and burst over edges
flowery sashes without restraint
eyes over an intricate trellis

decorous and inviting
pompadour eyes
voluptuous memories

pervade frothing libido
genital in hand

eyes dance to music of pipes and horns
throngs of satyrs dance

nymphs and heroes eyes
pelt garlands of roses

eyes
drip heavy ornamental waters
onto jolis derrières

pretending to be a dog eyes
a revolt against reason

rub honey
the naked shepherdesses
on shepherds lusty eyes

kiss them passionately
upper lips curl

tremble with excitement
an ancillary frisson

a destruction of naiveté
quivering eyes
that eye

II

Tormenting a Satyr

wonderful dream face
eyes full and green-blue-black
puffy
blue-rimmed hemispheres

pièce de résistance
to the hilt

with an ardent broth
mounds and folds

new joys
dance pompadour dance
prancing from couch to couch

tinkled with excitement
like young lambs in fresh spring

eyes responding like a flatterer
waxed fast and furiously
ravishing and stretching and
rumpling and crushing

nozzling wildly in the crevices

color and a complicated blurriness eye
moon had finally mounted

disarray disarray disarray

hair falling loose
soft delicious swollen

nervous and responsive and impassioned

effeminate stallion
gallant kiss rostrum

three-headed bitch
kitty hell eyes

loud
the heart knocks
exhausted lover

fishnet
fish not
no hysteria unrealized
none uncalculated

please no hysteria

no drudgery
eye hoots
spinning
spinning

dynamic load
an effulgent re-collection

mad carnival of frenzied intensity
delirious vernacular

idiotic thoughts

                                                becloudedbespreaded
mesmeric
myopic

shivering petard, of course
now bleached and liquidated

ravishing chandelier moments
what rosy reluctancies

ghostly reverberating structure of love
configurations of cumming
and disappearing

missingness
of excess
un-restrained but seemingly innocuous

into the finest of differences

erotic
gesticulations moved
a chromatic progression
decorated in

obbligato

this lure
this lure

mesmeric

blackness begins to snicker with delight
art as a vehicle for self-transcendence

nonsense eyes
total surrender...............mesmeric eyes
recitation of the mantra

rainbow bodies
hardwood bodies

vigorous throng chant
perched at the circumference

field of vision goes black
tunnel vision again sets in
details if desired

in eyes

corresponding dimensions
in the imaginary
transformation of the image

waves of electronic energy
and immaterial signals

this imaginative territory stretches
lost
in an infinite navigation

disappearing in the play of eyes

repeating itself ad infinitum

mesmeric with its descriptions
explanations
and commentaries

so strong
so ominous
inhumanly beauty eyes

desire and restlessness
duplicating eggs, sperm, and blood

into the area of unconscious
switch out of the passive mode
immersive
emergent mesmeric eyes

a redemption
and redefinition dive
wild and uncontrolled

breaking free of negative power
the order of earlier sex experiences

mesmeric things to all
often simultaneously

embodies smart intelligence
focus dirty unpredictability

consumption

possible recollection
system of intelligent orgasm

eyes costume
predetermined zones

hinder no psychic
expressions

oh, really?
billionth
rejoinder in understanding
cleanses and purifies

bowed over ever so deeply
mesmeric eyes

a malicious delight gave rich tonality
running on by itself

through dreamy usage
baroque play mesmeric eyes

the creation of unforeseen
seemingly automatic

spontaneously inventive vision
under a moment of
annihilation

independently of time space

abstract attempt at eliminating eye time

that famous castration allegory
of departure, of loss and of mythical return

frigid and forbidden
eyes containing the quest
of instantly crossed frontiers

strange affiliations
of symbolic replacements

lubricous daydream open eyes

within a circle
a horizontal point of view
analogous to cluster sex eye

a plethora of possibilities
like a dark eye machine creating pure repetitions
mesmeric eyes

hollowing out the void
accumulated movement
without pause
pelted with roses
declaring ravishing
the great quivering bottom

fasted upon by the throng
saturating the manifold lovers
with warm champagne douches

mesmeric eyes

fêtes gallantes merveilleuses

of eye world culture
a bawdy creature
under the influence of the high

swirling
phantasmagoric
delirium and delirium
higher and higher
faster and faster
eyes eyes eyes

encapsulating entire divine feminine
a ruffled disposition hounding a whittle
the thousand heads of eternity
a tiny open bird cage

whirl pool sucker
magnificence glistening
the grandeur

the grandeur

in a sea of glitter

eyes masquerade as humility
arrogance
eyes masquerade
hewn of tears

                              eyes masquerade
                        magnificence glistening
                              eyes masquerade
                              as a sea of glitter

                          pressing the crack of eyes

                          all tassels and grand folds
                                        a slow rite

                          weighted down with gold
                                ancient in meaning

                                     mesmeric eyes
                                   as beautiful as is
                                inhumanely possible

         painted, powered, gorgeously bewigged
                   like a marquis in a comic opera
                           heavy eyelids painted rose
                                     inexorable web
                                teasing proliferation
                               mesmeric eyes unable

                             unable to escape the potency
                               unable to voluptuously
                                 jealous with attention
                               able with mock severity

                    a little flagellation might be in order

                                     blushed with excitement

an amorous fessée
marvelous wine was dancing circuitously
frills that concealed the swell of able eyes

that twinkling consciousness
negations turned to affirmations

chaste
little new moon
precise and delicate

hung pale in the afternoon sky
meet some faraway darkness

enigmatic doors

secret cellars

walled garden of mesmeric eyes

warm and windless

bit of scented liqueur

combined aromatic pleasure

eyes lost in
a reverie
paintings accessible and banal

making less and less sense
scatological and

decadent

eyes going deeper and deeper
lanes and alleys of flesh

that rosy light
which only couples in love know

eyes unable nosegay
sweet danger
the peeping voyeur

a little frission of delicious alarm
unable mesmeric eyes
eyes clasped together
but not penetrated

swelling exaltation
unconquerable
eyes intoxicating one another

the spot of red flesh
from which tears flow
mesmeric nosegay

where eyes can seem endless

III

Secret Love of Dimness

snake on your shoulder

an astonishing secret

self
dramatizing

access boundless
half-sealed eyes

ethereal boundary

ambrosial odors of hair
with
equal languor

artistry with
verisimilitude

tormenting supposition

art no longer authentic?
just eye subjugation

notion bundled to an end?
ogle the unattached nosegay
thrown from several directions

part of a grand diva
little love notes
concealed in the blossom eyes

the hyperspace of simulation
making significant gains
kisses burning kisses

burning eyes sparkled
little inflaming attouchements
rêverie slowed the passage of time

dense body divulgence
accepted wisdom burning
burning some kind of lock

administratively
psychologically

everyone and everything in step
a sort of religious terror
the sexual fury of the goddess inherent
no history, no meaning, no conscience, no desire

all alone
fingering around some vague and
unrestricted burning ocular environment
withdrawing and closing itself

circular space at the periphery
an infinitely attenuated
and
adipose entry

sexual diversity and intellectual depth
oversteps and threshold of critical flesh
ancient and arcane eyes

burning

as illusory, as nameless, as unnamable, as
fraudulent

as unpredictable

mental, intuitive and psychic
hypothetical erudition burn

wind swept hills

beaches, high mount peaks, high towers
cork screws and
proclivity

effulgent yellow, crimson, blue-white
blade, cerebral balls
myrrh
pansy, primrose, vervain, violet

feeling, hotness, passion, blood, juice, life

pleasure
prophylactic destroying
purifications bonfires
abode fire eyes

burning candle flames, orbs
gold, crimson, orange, white of the sun's noon gay

hibiscus, mustard, nettle, onus, red peppers, cherry eyes
in flower burning

serpents
lions, horses
when their horns inflame sparks
feelings, fornications, firmness
daring, torment
inflamed sea nymph
the spout

drowsiness, kitty, streams, and rivers, springs and wells
intuition unconscious

proclivity womb
breeding fertility

lotus, mosses, rushes, seaweed, pool lilies
liquid pitch of coral snake

billow mammals, water-dwelling snakes
all eyes inflamed

creatures eyes and dandy bird eyes

flesh, expansion
fission
accumulation
creativity
bloody eyes

curtain flame, silence, chasms, caves, caverns
groves play shimmy with unused stones

tan, youthful, milky inflamed
baroque obelisk

rich man
sack, seed of chaff
transformation switch

everywhere and nowhere
within and without
the void

immoderation of eyes

duration, all spread
arching sprocket eye

phallocratic exchanges
entered upon the scope of attachment

physical and mental couple
opened up something inside

primed and primed
this delicious satyriasis

love off in a corner
leeway near to climax

hung back, as if reluctant
in fact only to sharpen the flame

desire

inflamed eyes

an agony of wantonness

of
impatience
of expectations

loving submissions pouring out
like some vast waterfall
ornate carpet
thinking ornate thoughtful eyes

golden ornate thread eyes
a curvaceous path

develop ornate designations
ornate genitals in hand

a lustrous pinkies cunx
cyclic in and out movements

breathing breathing
breathing
pulse beat ornate
genitals in ornate hand

rich void of repletion
luxuriate and luxuriated

lying like ornate drunks
ornate genitals in hand

loosened the sails
driven to siesta like
rams to a corral

                                    draw breath
                                     breathing
                                  genitals in hand

             heel and strain and then gather ballast
                                shining path extended
                                ornate genitals in hand

                                 periodic scratch marks

                                    the center as egg

            dividing space into an indistinct sprouting
                       had never known what ornate love was

                                       surrender
                           to yield, to abdicate and receive
                                       ravishing
                                       trembling
                                   genitals in hand

                             plunge deeply into a nexus

                                  without constraint

                                    to the flowers

                                   genitals in hand

                             shining line straight south
                        branch aligned with the co-ordinate
                                  tongue to the west

draw vertical dilly

horizontal dilettante

boas
perpendicular to the first
each kisser divided into four
genitals in hand to the flowers

genitals moaned softly
glistening

a pillar of numbers

consequences
were serpentine

persist flowers persist
to the flowers flailing

fragility more striking
like wind whipping through the foliage of a tall tree

imbroglio produced by the fathomless movement
to the flowers genitals in hand

gathering up dolphin eggs
walking an extenuated rainbow

delicious copula of lust
stamped by the sign of the ram

in one cathartic expenditure

rainbow genitals in hand

IV

Something Effulgent

glistening current
smiling in accord
without measure
and wholly paired

superlative glistening
glistening irremediably
in one cathartic expenditure

rainbow imp gone out the bottle

lingering and twirling and probing finger

embouchement
nonchalance

incubus refusals
to abdicate
to glistening

deep desire mingled with remorse
hungry for an antidote

a psychic one
a bone and flesh enact

harmony in desire
truly sensitive in the preparation

the hate had dulled
psychic genitals in hand

tissue of kisses and caresses
spool
as if there were no floor to it

this feverish disquisition
the sensibility, the sentiment

contingent, not eternal
prose rather than poetry

desire as fragile as fine wine

both psychic composites
which can achieve aesthetic value
like a bird's nest

kissbound in honeysuckle toil
a gallant cortège it must have seemed
tremulous and expectant
tasseled codpiece

such a flutter
such a flutter to the sounds of little suckings

still cobwebbed in the drowsiness
afternoon rendezvous

ephemeral
fluttering eyes
genitals in flutter hand

perfectly assured rhythms
overlaid with trills

and
appoggiaturas
as tender as a lake at twilight
tender
genitals in hand

beautiful unfinished things
little scraps of poetry

plucked rosebuds
and tender fiery love eyes

further into
the tender panopticon

at its core
tending eyes
an exquisite little quiverous path

this quivering ocular sea
like a stalk of fresh asparagus

whip tip of yellow watered silk
a suave and active finger

now sad, pensive and resigned
now more beautiful than ever

an airy scallop shell suspended
ties of affection quiver

like heroes doing so

quivering

genitals in hand

some delicate tracery hanging
distraction seemed endless

sallied forth a great pink
melee waiting

with many whispers and amorous murmurs

spirits flurried

quivered the charming nymph-guide

through a wee door
of tapestry dim passage

frolics and romps and
bagatelles and folasteries

endless roués and rouées
endless accouterments

foaming and billowing
the dimpled derrière

palming and persuading
endless fanciful endeavors

complete with dramatic éclat

low hum of bees
absorb pantomimes

operetta joys
the physical body endless

a vital step

uttered naughtiness
an immersive initiation

the sound of cooing cries
~~~~
smacked lips

all under a very blue and high sky

on a golden and red colored ornamental carpet
two goat-men

lighthearted
endless

surrounded by a sapphire sea
silk
nightdress tiptoed quietly

visualize a blue sphere lighting up
between your rear cheeks

sending a thread of light
endless genitals in hand

straight line from the head-hole to either
lighting up in the throat

a thread of light to the second point
tiptoed

~~~~~~~~~~~~~~~eeeee

in a slightly lower tone

perambulate

center of the cavity

sending its light to the third tiptoe

~~~~~~~~~~~~aaaaaaaaa
~~~~~~~~~~~~aaaaaaaaa

lower than the previous eyes
no sound of blood rushing

only the rumbling tiptoe

vision the thunderbolt fragmenting
with a tremendous roar

sending sparks into and through
beautiful rumbling eyes

fade

and the objects take up new positions

on a thick pile of magnificent
oriental carpets

rumble harmoniously around
the space

gradually condensed

prolonging itself through the wine
marcs
and armagnacs

without anything indecorous
rumbling

dark saturine eyes shifted
the spuriously romantic
shift on my guard

in the grip
brilliant moon poured its molten light into the lakes

shifty eyes turned ink-black
quick silver
according to angle

eyes as sexy waterlilies
the waves of tenderness

shifted
full of thrilling convulsions

of pleasures
lulled

melancholiness
joyous

slowness
breath

an air
of menacing furry
naked maidens drowning in snakes
a tiny boat scudding
through the mountainous surge

tossing among the huge waves
whose foam curled slowness
behind and before

severed genitals were
thrown slow to eyes

a terrified kitten mewing and rubbing
the twisting pussy
lurches itself free
gave birth to lovelier (if twisted) images

on a sun struck slowness
nothingness around the edges
full of weird ocular shadows

patches of meaning floated up from the vertigo
penetrating vision which turns people into masks

hollow organ which tries to resist
into caricatures with names
cover in body butt eyes

blown
blown out the ocular

candles
swan
waves of horror pass

sunk in gloomy lethargy
beneath the open silk robe
to resist
then offers
itself

opens up

and produces eyes
of
swan
slowness

slow
slow

connoisseur of ocular slowness

blissful and gargantuous eyes
stained by more than a million

in responsive nervous excitement
in pleasant reunion

shapes of prehistoric ocular women
ornamental gardens behind

threading the maze of gigantic gloomy woods
oaks and beeches cast their shadows around

ancient
willows writhing

roots strewn the ground like great
horrid melancholy snakes
pique part dark
in the form of an ocular uterus

loving with suave gestures
oh thousand varieties of desire

refresh ourselves

eyes still shaking

V

That Was How the Day Went By

amorous cupidons and caryatids
an elegance altogether attractive

luxuriated
in sentiment

embellished with loops, tassels, fleurons and formalized
heraldics

portiérs of dusty pink velvet

softly domed and figured with wreaths and curlicues
of heavenly cum

the floor sloped down revealing a discernable
but
minuscule nude

the pit had been closed
cream and everything

appreciation, smiling retorts
creamy suggestive grimaces

imaginary cream ejaculations
a buzz of comment and criticism

light had changed to a deep rose
enticing sounds of playful slaps

one of sensitive intimacy

the curtain parted
amber flesh
smooth pattern of mysterious eyes

buzz figures played
a dryness of spilt blood

~~~~~~~~~~~~mmaaaaaaaaa

saline consciousness
fed upon a certain secretion

continuously fine
and spicy

alchemical concept of égréore
eminently real at some point

inside of everything and everyone

useless to flog a spent snake
that certain nuts tended to secrete

parsimony apart
sprawling on the floor
absolutely bereft of even one drop

of perfect intensity
those buzzed eyes

perfect intensity
working out of the fantasy

of the containment mentality

in halting locutions
and with much syntactical awkwardness

this fresh beautiful afternoon
did dimly sprawl

did tongues smoothed out

did imagine take fire

an enticingly hidden radical
open-minded eye

imagination secreted and took fire
aplomb secreted with aplomb

aplomb took fire
in speechless adoration

eyes in awe and dexterous
celestial wine secreted
and took fire

eyes stabbed blindly
in transubstantiation

into the flaming eye spicy

some very heavy
lubricious action

the piquant lunar realm
no puedo mass

bien tu cacho gusano
chupas la vida vampiro
adentro mas

oral openness

be founded
previous romantic feel

collapsing realistic depiction
but self-love

self-acceptance

collapsing eyes took fire

through thick woods
to an antediluvian dwelling
a thick field all the traces

an exposed sword dripping
collapsing with blood

passed through a corridor to a colonnade
a garter belt
and mantle

red silk
the letter of blue velvet

lined with cherry silk
took spicy fire

pinkish watered-silk
lined erotically
appealing
collapsing images
eyes about to begin

in innocent robes of white silk
embroidered with gold
red and blue flowers

with flower buds
about to begin

elaborately embroidered eyes
a flaming candelabra

hand burned
a taper of reddish wax
a bouquet about to begin

a bell tinkled in
sprang a canopy of peach silk
a bell tinkled in

port opened at a trumpet peal
a harbinger advanced
splendid bouncing

splendid elaborate bouncing

an unseen calliope played

harmonizing sounds
of exquisite
yet robust, taste

holding the points high
chanting exorcisms

a sufferable panic

maudlin
manipulative mythologies
sweat profusely

appeared endless eyes
a litany in rhythmic line
milky-breast slashing down
milky-breast bearing an elaborate urn

pantheistic fascination
in a peculiar manner

a complete squeeze

the chime tinkled in the archive

a horn-shaped cup
of whitish liquid

an empty flask curiously shaped

aroma was musty

the dames
and hamadryads began a long litigation

a rich fiery opal
in which flames of light danced

quivering
quivering eyes

gleefully
then danced
tracing the patterns
a fantastic blossom of abundance

eyes moved round continuously
parted lips
instigating a shower of glistening

eyes drop from above
eyes
fell swooned

chime again tinkled
nymphet
cognizant

the organ
thundered forth majestic

cognizant of the eyes
glistening throes of erotic transport

both ballast and feeling
as the chime tinkled anew

wood floor strewn with petals and cut flowers
other hand being lost

griffins
 bees and griffins
eyes and more eyes glistening

mixing maypole mendacity
maypole flower maidens
swirling maypole tinkle
tinkled the depth of forgetfulness
perched on a tongue like rock

moonlight
not recognized
just tinkled

eyes hungry for love
quantitative
qualitative

automated indexing

 immense space nymphet

nymphet vagina dentate

conflict

incompatibility

or compulsion

mapping expectation
as melody
in theatrical memory

of necessity follow
incompatibility
or compulsion

eyes resist nothing
maneuvering through
tinkled encryption
encryption theater
assertion toward feeling
of moist and
wet expanse

maiden psychology
emphasis nymph
maiden machine
eyes tinkled

eunuchesque tendency eye

interfaced
gynander
lying antithetical

lying antithetical or simply
eunuch nymphet of
automatic ruling eyes

maiden vehicle
for unconstrained field
for those who prefer to play with ideas

less ego
more art
more tinkle

invariably found intolerable

pathway merging
immense
elevated eye parlor

burnished
upshot
with what felt like a riding crop

gracious
lubricated
proficient finger stroke
unconstrained tinkle slide

pulled
and twisted
buzzing like a bee
buzzing like a bee

off into the stratosphere

balmy accumulation
tink
smile

the monumental fur

auto raison
half-naked and danced

honeyed goblet paired a loft

hearts like a shiver
stirring the flanks
of a tinkling stallion in rut

destroyer of darkness
attain no velvet movements
nor
ritual or ceremony

feeble imitation
now in the languor of satiety

nymphet

trance

then faded to black

then faded to black

then the soft male eyes

capricious, weak, and withered
dependent, barbarous, deceived

non-beloved
vagina
dentate

where passion goes
to gratuitous ecstasy

drink of the nectar
of all
beneficent

gratuitous
gratuitous ecstasy
taken loosely

in it eyes lurk

no secret subtlety
and of utterance

voluptuous fire

cell's receptor
become subordinated
a ceaseless movement

a place of eyes
insert the genetic coding

insert this over and over
insert capricious eye
insert eyes
insert
capricious of pestilent

and
acrimonious desire

as fatal and sensuous
maiden scent

the dizzying array

within ergo
these imaginative
desires

teeming advances

shift and dissemble

urge images
shift and dissemble

capriciously

pursue their own strategies
astride this goat eye

yield viral particles
capricious cells in search of their own

discharges from the pressure

escape can be a painless fleeting

the internal pressure of many

maiden desideratum

modicums blown out of unheard of pleasures

milky-breasted insatiable soil
the darkest reaches of the bed
breasted bottomless crevasses

vex me
my eyes

harmonious code
vex me
fermented grapes of bacchic inebriation

cruelty
the fettering of the capricious hand
dead and no thought dies
fléche phallique eyes

eyes smeared with blood
caught up in a prosaic
materialistic world

entertain ye
with a little nymphet
understanding
downloaded yearning
capricious yearning yearning
nymphet
consciousness eye

from the matrix of animosity

purged from the dire
war between the sexes

no longer goat-in-the-machine
but machine-as-goat eye

across the linking medium
in a cloned disguise

come upon a honey flood
endlessly proliferate

ego is desire
so everything is ultimately desired

and undesirable

ever a preliminary forecast

eyes of terrible dissatisfaction
hidden

under the capricious nymphet
honey flood
under the nymphet
honey flooding
in dark perfume

ever what you were
eyes
eyes eyes

ever what you were
encircled with the tender aureole
of eternal beauty

ever what you were
eyes
eyes
eyes

teeming with goatishness purport

milky breasts float and heave

eyes floated and heaved
in the form of a cuckoo

born from your forehead
an image of flesh

a cloud shaped body
bent back under the moon's rays

pale light envelop
of liquid-white breasts

a silver mist
a capricious yes
shimmered
tenderly

afire
with red

moistened honeyed pussy

glistened the polished floor

perfume explain itself
an *amour à quarte pattes*

capricious eye extravagance

swaying, oozing, curling
eye tongue speak

ultimate extravagant touch stone
the sentience of our own body

sexual incubus
simply emptied

a caterpillar of self-doubt
hide your prick in your dreams

aromatic perfume
rolled about the dark winged chimera bacchante
ambitious in the realm of extravagance

amorous appetite
kindled by the waves of perfume

now rose and subsided
wobbled and merged and
deliquesced

with wild intense something
aficionado intellectuality

glittering extravagance

the nymphet eyes
roamed the labyrinth
masquerading

bovine guise

take your full pleasure
the extravagance wild

sense of jubilation
these proclivities in run

the margins of a lake
sun came up like a metallic laurel

looking sideways to see
nude reflection racing through the spear

regal heat spilled extravagance
beneath my feet

swift
dispelling the heavy dew

balls
in icy brilliance

proclivities veered
sharply to the right
consumed again
in
inexplicable joy

sun fire by a million
silver drops of prismatic light

onto wet eyelashes

the play of light
a contraction of the heart
the dark wet fingers

proclivitie touched eyes
circle like corolla

flower
floating into the silence
an ancient sun with bends of water
eyes
clinging naked

bodies in an esoteric act of lustration
like an extenuation

swelled my bough with the sap
proclivities of springtime eye

eyes bristling with desire
eyes sweating from this branch

fluids of obscene virility
eyes of vast proclivities

rump
against the moist down of thy branch

water, swans, grandiose pagan fables

such are the cheap thrills needed
to shock the bourgeoisie

VI

Awful Daring

        that imprudent moment's
        surrender

our glittering and liquefying multiple reflections
    nostrils quivered in ardent palpitations

        sputter and fade
        sputter and fade

the ecstatic numbness that makes proclivities
        a trifle insincere

        self-flagellation
        no
        greater joy

        spectacle of creamy
        quivering bosom
        heaving belly

        ideal tossing thighs
        set off against the tiger skin

a swan like crown of red passion flowers
        gold pit viper round

        naked arm
        haughtily and lubriciously
        fingering the sorry eye hole

        circumlocation
        a torn and

scattered rose
amorous of thy body
and
of thy seed

athirst
for thy sperm

thy body wine and apples
pliant cock vein fire

enchantress
lips athirst
brought little

half closing eyes
bent back under moon rays

flicked
humid
salty tip

slip athirst down
between breasts and gently flick

honey dripping
and supercilious centaur flicking

resurrection lacerated
athirst into nakedness
all creation but thyself

washed in vertigo

goat of lubricity
thine own sake self-love
air something my eye
like the beaming of vast vulva wings

be flown now
athirst

vulval castle crave
athirst
for thorny path

some coherent
understandable
explanation

mere epiphenomenon
brilliant and disdainful

darling
heart-gripping creature

enchantress dreaming
so chestnutty

so musky
full of sadness and of
fortuitousness

wishing it might last forever

moaning

to bolster these mountainous words

sapience and wisdom
of
disenchantment
wishing it might last forever

wish-wobbled city bells rang

like the tongues of memory
like the deep primeval grotto
like the water sprite explained

faint artist engraving eyes

thirsty for
fragility kisses

scribbled their way
down dignity divined

separating heaven and earth
from the artistic

eyes breathing in chime
very softly

going up and down

rhythmically
rhythmically
rhythmically

rhythmic eyes
felt the sensual drive
and
accepted it

myriad forms
very softly
very
breath quickened

essentially like rut
in direct apprehension

no intermediaries
no
conventional protocol

often outré
unconventional

out of touch
dreaming inebriated eyes

flower of the sea's deepest garden
a thirst for bewildering solitude

enveloped in timidity
and
darkness

splintering your vision
grotesquely slipping

one foot ahead of the other
an exhilarated lover

eyes searching and challenging
fists of orgiastic transport

a whole new world of color
in flounces and flowers

maypoles skip in circles around
blue swimming hole within
maypole monstrous wirling d'art

take up a bloodied stake

the goat-footed boy-satyr of ancient myth
play
exquisite flute

and sing exquisite
into the earth a bestial
disembarrassment

bouts of lewd and reckless dancing
ear and eye strange heavy

petal-headed flower maiden

exquisite
uncontrollable eyes

existence of thee in your phallocentricity

fearsome production of desire

treasures of their many breasts
prima facie consciousness

exquisite necks opened
then like naked flesh
run

an exquisite moisture of silken smoothness
slip mover of night
thou loin-clutcher
many-breasted
magnanimity of self-love
transcend ecstasy by ecstasy

shoulders
fruit, flowers and star cross
highly aroused rows of bosoms

quivering soft
as cotton
into this eye

quivering greater
exultation

probing
kneading

every last
exquisite breast

eyes
quivering
arching and suck

honey quiver pouring
undulating like waves

quivering
touching the very depths

fall in hot love
absorber of the sun

the self doth not desire
neither day nor night

eyes penetrating all things
inexplicably

exquisite hoary
deep eyes
dark
illimitable

orchard ocean
without bound
without dimension

under the moon's oblique paleness

olive trees
and almond trees spread

tangled limbs assume the tortured arch

swaying
twisting

passionately spreading their legs
glistening on the floor in a pool of perfume

trembled hands and knees
hovering over the moist
exquisite eyes
of open flower
rush of intensity
exhaled
in great warm breaths
powerful smell of beautiful dripping
numerous breasts
outthrust

belly
swelling under the moon
drunk
exquisite
yes

rays of the sun pierced
dreaming

into orbit around itself
ecstatic

in the generosity of self-loss

pleasures
of a self without end

absorb self-enhanced energies
rigorous opposition
of subject and object

ecstatically open to pivotal reflexive surface
now unconscious in their self-simulation

great warm breaths
powerful beautiful drippings
never be unmasked
exquisite pain of embellishment is enduring
swooning pain of embellishment is enduring

of moist and fertile earth
hast atavistic retrogressions

wallowing in aplenty

dark grotto eye

warm inviolate womb

dark palpitating expanse

revealing a deep cavern
of carnal knowledge
and opulence

align beauty
with transformative eloquence

in the revealing eyes
and talking eyes

that carnal persona walking
in sauté abstractivity

eyes sudden drop lubricated front
thou magnificent belly
slid down

the inconceivableness that transcends
eyes
revealing human desire

incongruous
sensation

thou hast not wearied

would thy pleasure

be wantonness

atmosphere dark
and slumberous
spent hours

caressing
the soft flesh neck throw shivers

magnified
mobile

and moving

naked on the floor and circle
an invisible hand has stretched

swollen
headless eyes
magnified images form
high buttock
courtesan revealed
made of elastic tissue

stretch and extend eyes
swell towards
mammoth breasts

part in an infeasible way

the sanguine
glistening
sex revealed

expanded
as if one had taken a tulip
and split it

archetypal moving
like rubber
convulsive gestures proceeding

a monstrous
orgasm

a seeing of electric reality

eyes will kiss all things and never sleep
fluttering poetic color of expansion

fluttering
deepened
the damp-saturated air

panicky
metastasis revealing
sharpened by the sea-reflected light

destined for a teat-à-teat

dreamy
tempered
radiance
teat-à-teat eyes looming
and ponderously grand

a body
with both mixture slowed

glowing pagan immanence revealing

semi-transparent
skin turned eyes

eyes as an atmosphere accentuated
transgressive sacred glowing eyes

eyes pagan immanence
festively put to deathless restoration
she-goat in full udder

boat-like new moon swam
swaying trees reveal
becomes limitlessness

she-goat watching yourself
watch yourself

revealing sexuality
haunted eyes

the mirror of moonlit multiple-selves
breath
of ribald lightning

absolute propinquity of the real
revealing eyes the same
thou whirlwind of desire
eye thou drunken chalice of ecstasy

becomes patterned afresh

she-goat was none other
model of self-simulation

also the time
of the end of time

the only time where myth could take place

                                              eye
                                             mood
                                      or condition
                                      or emotion

           absolute necessity regarding our loving
                                  excite cause and effect
                                     without any appeal

                                   association permitting
                                               inclusion
                                       before conception

                                                    ego
                                            appreciation

                                          or universal
                                              laughter

                                  the principle that allows
                              palpably transfigured before
                                   this onslaughting climax
                                                    naiad
                                        dressed in nothing
                                 but blue fake-fur stand

                                      take for the weaving
                                              usurpation

                                        every libertine
                                  conversation infected

paradigmatic eye assumptions
no more revealing

than

glossy eyed
assertions

VII

As We Know. As We Know

western crack a ruddy full moon
babbling like a femme fatale

naiad
dressed in nothing
red fake-fur appears

corner of a scarlet veil
wind raised against the evening sky

mirror
reflecting the setting sun

veil
trembled like a flame in sublimity

imaginative veil
trembled like a flame

spectral head bowed
moving

eyes with infinite grace
and majesty

outer steps
which wound
like a spiral round

fiery afterglow
reddened pearl necklace
high vermilion tower

as if to be transcended

eyes like a river of ruby pleurisy
ye now
the ecstasy within

all mouths and fingers and tongues
big mouth
seeking nippled clitoris

a slew of uncertain signs swarming
mesmericly
hinting at an all-inclusive eye

up along the great purple wall
triggering off an endless succession

the abstraction of self-love
towards the abjection of nullity

without even asking

mounted glory resplendent
the magnificence of velvety maroon

eyes like silk fabric

instituted single finger assiduity
shuddering moistened open eyes

eyes leaped forward

an endless contraction
heaved inside

like great grotesque, quivering blobs of color

sea-maiden arose oscillating

shivering brightly
brightly shivering

summer sprites revealing
revealing
shivering brightly

revealing the cool
revealing
aromatic wall

scurrilous seats drew fresh ardor
revealing points westward

they became
pusillanimously
eyes revealing uninterrupted

multiple mouths and hands
loquacious hands of lassitude

twinkling tongues in hair
shuddering

excess will be our excuse for being
connoisseur of embellishment

shuddering eyes strive
to do the same

twinkling theoretician

be breathlessly put into oscillation

all the doubles implode
explored from an inward region of strangeness of feeling
defiance through ecstasy

therapeutic
and salvational in turns

the shape of an élite beehive

there are no divisions
only voyeuristic continuity of sensation

and daemoniacal creativity

shuddering urge
will be satiated by the intelligent
a complication of spatial levels

leave no fixed sardonic planes of reference
snake eyes covered with

escutcheons

chant in a soft exotic lingua
combatant headband

the cobweb torque of gold

shudder loosened ribbon
intelligential and unashamed

absolute silence
rapt in an indulgent haze

lost to everything
a calliope rolled forth
some heavy shudder

diminutive
and chivalrous

an arduous tension between
two loosened ambitions

loosened
eccentric

expressiveness
loosened desire for beauty

naiveté came to a halt

the demonstrative divergence loosened

haughty

naiveté

dynamic

a nominal
singleness loosened

haughty voluptuous eyes
loosened

over the sea and the garden
moon poured down its stream of light

the delicate influences of lunar water
stirring light-footed voiced fairies

desire
naught but love
loose and dank

the hallway bathed in total darkness

love
naught but love

fallow and languid and
splendidly empty

lascivious, lewd
and depraved

invisibly and presently

slowly

loosened

VIII

Weary From Solitude

white flowers in the garden
the wind shaking the house

the apparition moved tenderly
bent the bow
to pierce the heart

chimeras
full of unwrinkled suavity
chimeras full of admirable aplomb

just down the hall
weary from solitude

grotesquely attenuated satyrs
wearing masks and
sporting bundles of roses tied to their privates

as immaterial horns and lips
mouth of dragons
and eyes of swans

poured scarlet red wine
frothed
anodyne concoctions

horns
and lips exercising charm

slow
full of hesitations and nuances

too beautiful to be really clever
offering little in the way of resistance

fais-moi mal chéri

like a grape trellis lambaster
weary from solitude

in honey
déchirez-moi
on garden balcony

in honey
kiss by kiss
bite by bite
howling
and
hurtling

melted at last
a single centaur
joined

melted at last

an ice-blue pool
chimeras

deep wantonness
and pitch

misplaced would be reminiscences

just lapses from satiety to indifference

> weary from solitude
> like an ancient discourse
> a salient discourse
> which goes on

as if passing from a satyr to a faun

IX

Never the Waggishness

clothed
only in the sound

dreaming in slogans and pictograms

releasing
of
disembodied fibula

losing the sexual rhythm

antlers growing on temples
full of delightfully perverse

full of kiss by kiss

went mad

full
an expression of eternal verity

explicitness
and nakedness

a resurgent atavism
based on obsession
impregnated by
sustained desires

void
responding to longing

supposition to deep recollection
full of
kiss by kiss by kiss by kiss

circumlocutions
its compliances

thus

sally forth
and be inordinate

projected like a beam kissed precious body
the ecstatic condition of revelation

by shear ecstatic power
kiss by kiss a functional activity

expressed in a symbolic vernacular
the desire towards ideal joy

somber
candle lit room
a slight trance with no particular maudlin conceits

kiss by kiss
deeper
and more remote

decadent overindulgence

a theoretical attack

the reification of consciousness
full of
kiss by kiss

with mercurial knowledge of
mise en scene
demeanor deep-memory

threatening the common order
full of
kiss by kiss

spiritual significance
as a studied self-abasement

an archimedean fulcrum
full of
kiss by kiss

sécheresses
vengeresses
castratrices

explicitly eschewing categorization

spectacle of mind-swamping consciousness
full of kiss by kiss

as dilettante folly
underlying everything

a web of connections

full of kiss by kiss

upon which we can exert
manipulative pressure
more than we are normally
led to believe possible

springing forth from the id
complex
entangled, erotic transfigured

the delicious copula of kisses
limpid
unruffled, respectful, and disengaged

full of convoluted compositions
kissed
vague
confiscations

full of the subtle
and infinite transformative possibilities
of love

kiss
by
kiss

Acknowledgments

The poem *Destroyer of Naivetés* owes relentless thankfulness to the too-much artists who helped inspire its ornate mannerisms: Ovid, Petronius Arbiter, Giacomo Casanova, Charles Baudelaire, Stéphane Mallarmé, Paul Verlaine, Arthur Rimbaud, Joris-Karl Huysmans, Raymond Roussel, Comte de Lautréamont, Tristan Tzara, Antonin Artaud, Gertrude Stein, Henry Miller, Jean Genet, Georges Bataille, Francis Picabia, Samuel Beckett, Allen Ginsberg, William S. Burroughs, John Giorno, Federico Fellini, Ken Russell, Jack Smith, Kathy Acker, Robert C. Morgan, Bradley Eros and Carolee Schneemann. They have all helped inspire its eccentric erotic sensibility and its self-consciously elaborate stylistic conceits; its pulsating euphuism. I dedicate it to my wife, Marie-Claude.

www.ingramcontent.com/pod-product-compliance
Lightning Source LLC
Chambersburg PA
CBHW020933180426
43192CB00036B/972

9780692573129